The Tiny Woman

1

The tiny little woman
lived in a tiny little house

2

with a tiny little parrot
and a tiny little mouse.

Every time the tiny little woman
tried to speak,

the parrot went **squawk** and the
mouse went **squeak**.

The tiny little woman
made them tiny little meals

of tiny little cakes
and tiny little eels.

And every time the tiny little
woman tried to talk,
the mouse went **squeak** and the
parrot went **squawk**.